FINDING OUT ABOUT HOLIDAYS

Ramadan

A Muslim Time of Fasting, Prayer, and Celebration

Carol Gnojewski

Enslow Publishers, Inc.

40 Industrial Road
Box 398
Berkeley Heights, NJ 07922
USA

PO Box 38
Aldershot
Hants GU12 6BP
UK

http://www.enslow.com

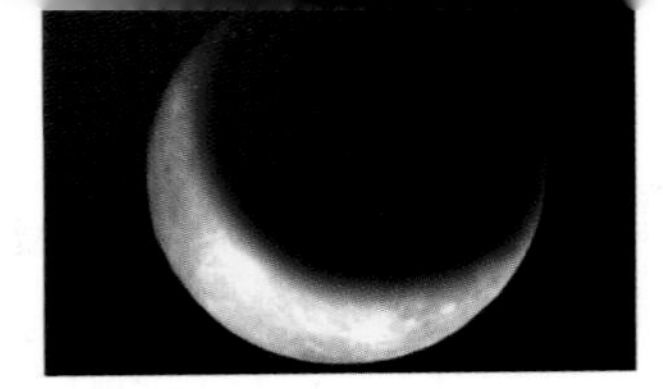

The editor would like to thank the Council on Islamic Education for their academic input.

Library of Congress Cataloging-in-Publication Data

Gnojewski, Carol.
Ramadan : a Muslim time of fasting, prayer, and celebration / Carol Gnojewski.— 1st ed.
v. cm.—(Finding out about holidays)
Includes bibliographical references and index.
Contents: Sky watch — Special message — Meet at the mosque — Ramadan routine — Eid festivities — Ramadan project.
ISBN 0-7660-2275-7
1. Ramadan—Juvenile literature. 2. Fasts and feasts—Islam. [1. Ramadan. 2. Fasts and feasts—Islam. 3. Islam—Customs and practices. 4. Holidays.] I. Title. II. Series.
BP186.4.G66 2004
297.3'62—dc22
2003027482

Printed in the United States of America

10 9 8 7 6 5 4 3 2 1

To Our Readers:
We have done our best to make sure that all Internet Addresses in this book were active and appropriate when we went to press. However, the author and publisher have no control over and assume no liability for the material available on those Internet sites or on other Web sites they may link to. Any comments or suggestions can be sent by e-mail to comments@enslow.com or to the address on the back cover.

Photo Credits: AFP/Getty Images, p. 38; AP/Wide World Photos, pp. 6, 11 (bottom), 31, 32, 42; ©1996-2004 ArtToday, Inc., p. 8 (top), 9, 10, 11 (top), 14, 26 (top), 28, 35, 37; © 1999 Artville, LLC., p. 15; Corel Corporation, pp. 4, 8 (bottom left and right), 12, 13, 16, 18, 19, 22, 24, 29, 34, 41; European PressPhoto Agency, EPA, p. 40; ©2001 HAGA Library Inc., pp. 26 (bottom), 30, 36; © 1996-2004 JupiterImages, pp. 1, 2, 3, 39, 46, 47, 48; Tony Kurdzuk/The Star-Ledger, p. 17; Matt Rainey/The Star-Ledger, p. 27; ©Peter Sanders/HAGA/The Image Works, pp. 7, 43; The Star-Ledger, pp. 20, 21, 23; Cathy Tardosky, pp. 44, 45.

Cover Photo: background, AFP/Getty Images; Inset #1, Corel Corporation; Inset #2, © 1996–2004 JupiterImages.

CONTENTS

The Islamic calendar is based on the moon's rotation around the earth.

CHAPTER 1

Sky Watch

Night has fallen on one half of the world. For nearly 2 billion Muslims—people of the Islamic faith—this night is special. Muslim children scan the sky eagerly. They are too excited to sleep. At moonrise, Ramadan, the ninth month of the Islamic year, begins. During Ramadan, Muslims spend the entire month gathering as families and communities. They celebrate with prayer, fasts, and feasts in honor of God (*Allah* in Arabic).

September is the ninth month out of twelve months in the solar calendar year. But even though Ramadan is also the ninth of twelve

THE ISLAMIC CALENDAR

In 2001, the United States Postal Service announced its plans for a special stamp. This is an Eid stamp, that celebrates the Islamic festivals marking the end of Ramadan.

These Indonesian Muslim girls are reading the Qur'an.

months, it does not fall each year in September. In the Arabic language, the word *Ramadan* means the "hot month." However, Ramadan may fall in the summer or winter. This is because the Islamic calendar follows the lunar calendar and the Western calendar follows the solar calendar.

The solar calendar is based on the number

of days it takes Earth to revolve around the sun. That is why there are 365 days in a solar year. As Earth travels around the sun, the amount of sunlight Earth receives changes. When Earth moves closest to the sun, it is summer in the United States. When it is farthest away

Muslims in India end the daily Ramadan fast with a group meal.

This diagram shows the rotation of the earth around the sun.

from the sun, we have winter. These changes help make the seasons. Our calendar follows the same seasonal changes every year.

The Islamic calendar, known as the *Hijri* (HIJ-ri) calendar, does not match the motion of the sun. It depends on the motion of the moon. This makes it a lunar calendar.

The sun always lights half of the moon. It lights the half facing the sun. As the moon

THE ISLAMIC CALENDAR

The twelve months of the Islamic calendar are Muharram *(moo-HUR-rum),* Safar *(SUF-er),* Rabi *(rub-EEY)* the First, Rabi the Second, Jumada *(joo-MAH-da)* the First, Jumada the Second, Rajab *(ra-JUB),* Sha'ban *(SHAA-bon),* Ramadan *(rah-ma-DAAN),* Shawwaal *(SHAW-waal),* Zul Qi'dah *(zool-KI-dah), and* Zul Hijja *(zool-HEEJ-jah).*

moves around Earth, we see different parts of it lit up. Sometimes we see no moon. Other times, we may see a crescent moon, a half moon, or a full moon. These are the moon's phases.

Muslims in olden days were great sky watchers and scientists. They noticed that a complete cycle of the moon lasts twenty-nine-and-a-half days. Each set of phases equals one month. There are 12 twenty-nine-and-a-half-day cycles, which makes a lunar year 354 days long. This matches what is written in the Qur'an, the Islamic holy book.

The lunar year is eleven days shorter than

This is how the moon appears as it rotates around the earth.

the solar calendar year. This is why solar calendar months and lunar calendar months begin and end at different times.

The moon's first phase is the new moon. No moon can be seen in the sky. It is hidden from view. The moon first becomes visible as a crescent. Islamic months begin the day after the sighting of the first crescent moon.

On the night before Ramadan, moon watchers wait. With telescopes and binoculars, they look for the moon.

When the moon appears like this in the sky, it means an Islamic month has begun.

Children in Egypt carry a *fanoos* (faa-NOOS), or lantern. A fanoos is made of tin and colored glass. It has a candle inside of it. Lighting a fanoos during Ramadan is a tradition that began over a thousand years ago.

The *caliph* (KAY-lif), or community leader, watched for the Ramadan crescent. The children of the town followed the caliph, lighting his path. They sang holiday songs as they swung their lanterns. When the bright crescent appeared, the children shouted. *Ramadan Mubarak* (ra-ma-DAAN moo-BAA-rek)! Happy Ramadan!

Some people use a telescope to spot the crescent moon.

An Egyptian family shops for a fanoos in a local market.

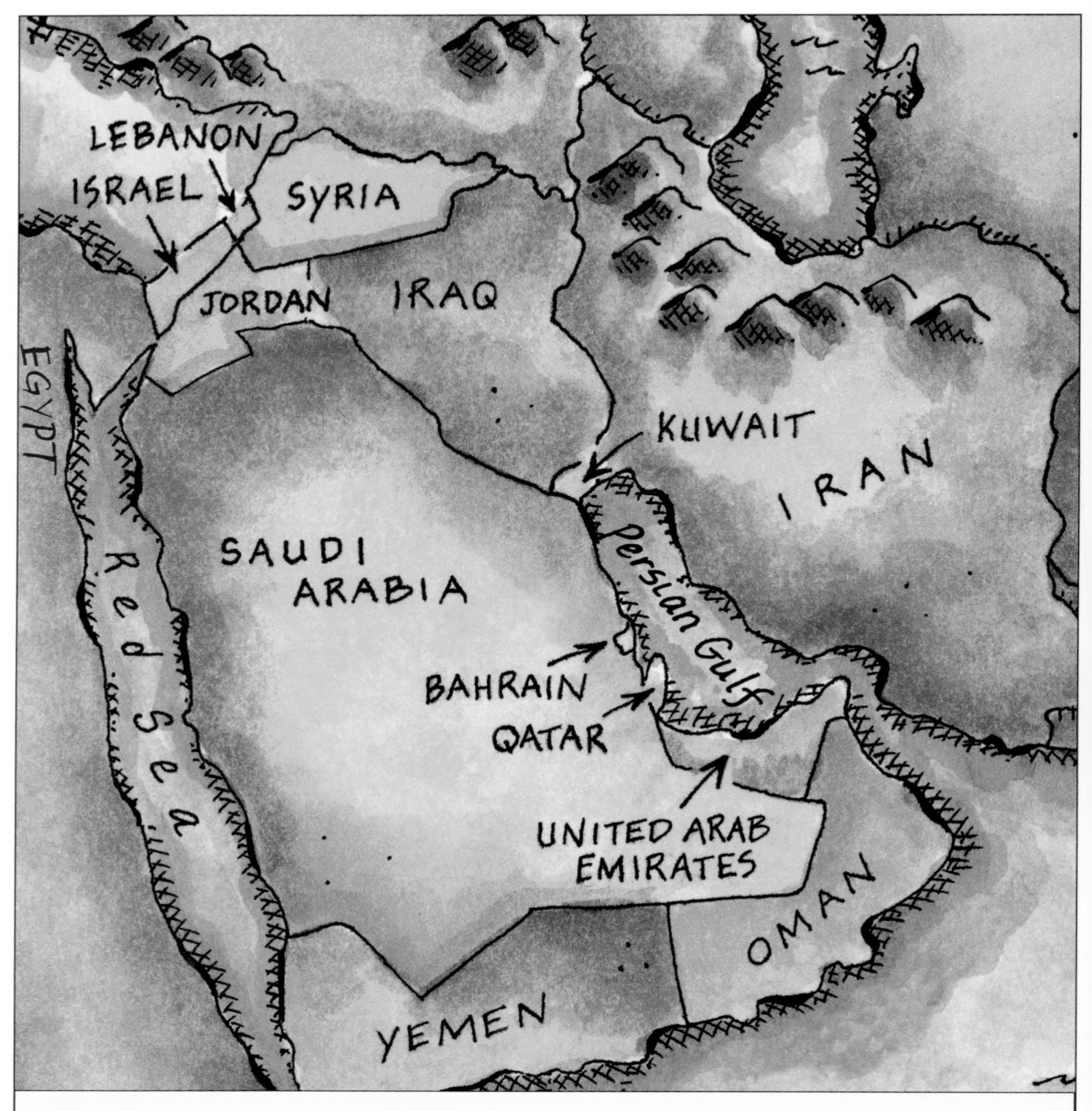

The Prophet Muhammad lived in what is now Saudi Arabia. It is a country in the part of the world called the Middle East. This is what the area looks like today.

CHAPTER 2

Special Message

In both the East and the West, calendars are arranged around important events in history. The Christian calendar centers on the life and death of Jesus Christ. It has been in use in many countries around the world since 1582. The Christian calendar was adopted for non-religious purposes. People around the world use it.

Time before the birth of Jesus is called B.C., which means "before Christ." Dates after Jesus's birth are labeled A.D. (*Anno Domini*)—"in the Year of Our Lord."

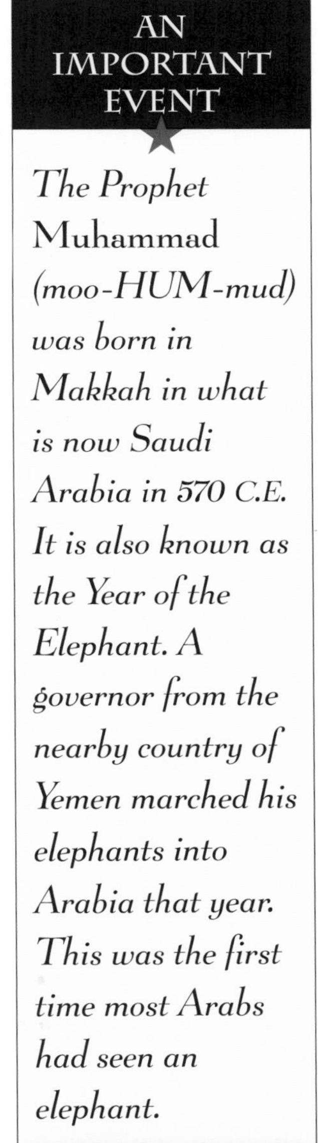

AN IMPORTANT EVENT

The Prophet Muhammad (moo-HUM-mud) was born in Makkah in what is now Saudi Arabia in 570 C.E. It is also known as the Year of the Elephant. A governor from the nearby country of Yemen marched his elephants into Arabia that year. This was the first time most Arabs had seen an elephant.

To make the calendar useful to everyone, the terms "before the common era" (B.C.E.) and "common era" (C.E.) were created. B.C.E. can be used in place of B.C., and C.E. can be used in place of A.D.

The Islamic calendar centers on the formation of the first Muslim community in Medina (also spelled Madinah). It was made in 638 C.E. by Muslims who believed they were

Muslims make their way to the Prophet's Mosque in Medina, Saudi Arabia.

Two boys sit on the edge of the Mountain of Light in Saudi Arabia.

part of the history begun by Muhammad's teachings about Islam. Dates on the Islamic calendar start from the year that the Prophet Muhammad moved from the city of Mecca (also spelled Makkah) to Medina in the year 622 C.E. This event is called the *Hijra* (HIJ-ra). Dates are labeled A.H., which means "after Hijra." Islamic dates are 579 years behind Western dates. The year 2003 C.E., for example, is the year 1424 A.H.

Saudi Arabia borders the Red Sea.

The Prophet Muhammad lived in what is now Saudi Arabia, a country in the Middle East. Deserts, mountains, and warm seas surround Saudi Arabia. It is a land of extremes. The weather is either very hot or very cold. There are deserts, marshy areas, small forests, valleys, and grazing land for livestock. During the time of Muhammad, Arabs lived in tribes. Wars and fights among tribes went on all the time. Most tribal people worshipped many gods and goddesses. Muhammad chose instead to worship Allah, the one God of his ancestor Abraham.

Every year during the month of Ramadan, Muhammad would travel to a cave called *Hira* (HEE-ra) in the hills near Mecca. According to Muslim belief, he went there to be alone with

God and to pray for guidance. The Angel Gabriel appeared before Muhammad when he was forty years old. This visitation happened near the end of Ramadan. In Arabic, the word "angel" is *malaa'ika* (ma-LAA-e-kaa). It means "conveyor," or "carrier." Muslims believe that angels are servants of God.

Angels are believed to be invisible to humans. They are thought to surround people

People today still pray the way Muhammad did.

at all times to guide and protect them. The Angel Gabriel is a special angel. His job is to give messages from God to holy people called prophets.

When the Angel Gabriel appeared before him, Muhammad became very frightened. The Angel Gabriel gave Muhammad the first of many messages. The angel asked him to read. But Muhammad did not know how to read or to write.

Muhammad was orphaned at the age of six. His uncle, Abu Talib, raised him in the city of

Muhammad worked as a shepherd while he lived in Mecca. A shepherd is a person who tends sheep.

Mecca. When Muhammad was young, he worked as a shepherd. As he grew older, Muhammad helped his uncle. He helped to carry goods across the desert on camels and horses. Later, Muhammad married a wealthy businesswoman named Khadijah, who admired Muhammad and proposed to him. She was fifteen years older than he was.

Muhammad helped his uncle carry goods for trade on camels across the desert.

When Muhammad received the message from the Angel Gabriel, he hurried home to Khadijah. He repeated what the angel had told him. Together, they asked her cousin, a scholar, for advice. He convinced Muhammad to accept the revelation that Gabriel had brought him.

Muhammad memorized God's words and presented them to the tribal leaders. Muhammad's message about worshipping one God and living peacefully was unpopular. The

Many people followed Muhammad's belief in one God.

leaders did not want to change the traditions that made them powerful. But many other people liked what Muhammad had to say. The Muslim population spread and outlasted the warring tribes. Now, Islam is the fastest-growing religion in the world.

Muhammad recited the message of Islam to all who would listen. Scribes wrote down these teachings. Before Muhammad's death, they were organized into a holy book called the Qur'an. The Qur'an is the primary source of Islamic teaching. Like the Christian Bible and the Jewish Torah, it is said to be the word of God. Written in verse form, the Qur'an reads like poetry. Speaking it aloud makes its graceful language more powerful.

The Qur'an is an important part of the Islamic religion.

According to Muslim tradition, the Angel Gabriel brought God's messages to Muhammad for twenty-three years. These revelations are organized into 114 chapters. The Qur'an was revealed in the Arabic language. Arabic is the language that Muhammad knew and understood. The Qur'an is written in Arabic script, and there are no pictures in it. Arabic reads from right to left, unlike English. To decorate the sacred text, Muslims often write

The Qur'an is written in Arabic.

the Arabic script in a fancy style known as calligraphy. Muslims all over the world learn Arabic so they can recite the Qur'an as Muhammad did.

Muslim children learn about the Qur'an and Ramadan in school.

Because Muhammad received the first passages of the Qur'an during Ramadan, it is a holy month for Muslims. Ramadan is sometimes called the Month of the Qur'an. The twenty-seventh night of the month is celebrated as the night he received his first revelation. It is called *Laylat-al-Qadr* (LAY-lat-al-CUD-er). This means "Night of Decree." The Qur'an is important because its teachings are part of a Muslim's daily life. In some Muslim countries, businesses and schools close on the twenty-seventh. This lets worshippers rest during the day to prepare for a night of prayer.

Mosques are where Muslims go to pray. This is the Blue Mosque in Turkey.

CHAPTER 3

Meet at the Mosque

Ramadan is a time of quiet thoughts and self-control. Throughout the month, Muslims follow the Prophet Muhammad's example by making an extra effort to think about life and to spend time alone with God. Muslims pray to God five times a day. These prayers are called *Salaat* (sa-LAAT). At dawn, midday, late afternoon, sunset, and in the evening, Muslims take time for ritual prayer.

During prayer, Muslims face towards the *Ka'bah* (KAA-bah), a cube-shaped building located in the holy city Mecca. Muslims believe it was built as a house of worship by Abraham

A PLACE OF WORSHIP

One way that Muslims show their commitment to God is by going to a mosque and bowing to God in worship. Mosques are holy places and are kept as clean as possible. Worshippers and visitors must take their shoes off before they enter a prayer area.

Since Muslims must pray throughout the day, sometimes they have to stop where they are and pray.

A prayer compass points in the direction of Mecca.

and his son Ishmael long ago. The direction of the prayer (facing the Ka'bah) is called *qibla* (KIB-la). The qibla varies depending on where one lives. In order to find the qibla, many Muslims use a prayer compass. This special compass looks like an ordinary compass. But, instead of pointing north, it points to Mecca. There are even prayer compass watches. The watch can automatically calculate prayer times, too. Prayer calendars and software programs also help to remind Muslims of their prayer schedules. This is important because

Muslims live all over the world and in many different time zones.

Before prayer, Muslims perform a washing ritual called *wudu* (wo-DOO). During wudu, Muslims cleanse their hands, mouth, nose, face, arms, and feet. This prepares Muslims for worship. Muslims stand, raise their arms, sit, kneel, and bow before God as they pray.

Muslims wash their hands, face, and feet before entering the mosque to pray.

The word *mosque* (MAHSK) comes from *masjid* (MUS-jid), a place for bowing low. *Muslim* means "submitter to God."

The prayer area in a mosque is a simple open space, usually carpeted. Special mats or prayer rugs often are used to mark the rows that worshippers form when praying together.

Some Muslims carry prayer beads that they use to recite praises to God. Most strands have ninety-nine beads on them. Each bead represents one of God's ninety-nine names, such as "The Forgiving," or "The Mighty."

Prayer services increase throughout Ramadan. Muslims may spend all day or night in prayer. Muslims are encouraged to pray together rather than alone whenever possible.

Muslims pray to mark the end of Ramadan in the front of a mosque in New York.

Muslims often pray together at a mosque. A mosque is a sacred place, like a church or a synagogue. It is a building that Muslims visit to remove themselves from the business of their day and to unite with other worshippers. An *imam* (ee-MAAM), or prayer leader, gives a sermon on Fridays. He leads prayer by reciting verses from the Qur'an in a songlike way. The other worshippers follow the imam as he bows before God.

Mosques are peaceful and beautifully designed. Some have smooth, flat stone roofs, while others have large painted or tiled domes called *qubbas* (KOOB-bas). The Prophet's Mosque is a famous mosque in Medina, Saudi Arabia.

The Dome of the Rock, a monument in Jerusalem, has a large painted dome called a qubba.

Many mosques have colorfully painted tiles with Arabic writing on them.

On each corner of the building stand tall, slender towers, or *minarets* (mihn-uh-REHTS). A caller, or *mu'adhin* (moo-ED-dhin), calls from the minaret to gather people for worship. The mu'adhin may use a microphone and a loudspeaker that reaches across town. In Cairo, Egypt, the government fires a cannon to announce the Ramadan prayers.

The inside of a mosque is organized and is simple. There are no statues and paintings inside a mosque. Instead, mosques are decorated with calligraphy and patterns of colorful tiles. Large courtyards and prayer halls may contain thick carpets, fountains, arches, and pillars. The Prophet's Mosque has enormous, electronic umbrellas in one of its courtyards. These umbrellas open when it rains to keep worshippers dry.

Some mosques hold an *itekaf* (it-e-KAF) as the month draws to a close. In Arabic, *itekaf* means "seclusion." It is a spiritual retreat that gives Muslims a chance to think about their goals and to become closer to God. Along with *taraweeh* (tur-ah-WEE-uh), or special night prayers in Ramadan, itekaf gives Muslims a chance to be with their fellow worshippers to share meals, to talk, and to learn from each other. For some Muslims, this night of togetherness builds excitement for the festive Eid ul-Fitr that takes place after Ramadan.

Muslims in Iowa end their day of fasting during Ramadan with a hearty feast.

These men in Pakistan are making a special kind of flatbread that is a common pre-morning breakfast during Ramadan.

CHAPTER 4

Ramadan Routine

The main duty of each Muslim during Ramadan is *Sawm* (SO-um), or fasting. Muslims rise before dawn and eat a hearty breakfast, or *sahur* (su-HOOR). Then, they do not eat or drink again until nighttime. The Qur'an says that followers may eat and drink at any time during the night.

Our bodies can survive without water for three or four days. You can survive without food for many weeks. It all depends on how much fat and muscle you have. Even so, think about all of the times that you eat meals or snacks during the day. Going without food and water for a whole

FIVE PILLARS OF ISLAM

The Five Pillars of Islam are important in Muslim life. These acts of worship include:

- Shahada *(sha-HAA-duh), or profession of belief in God*
- Salaat *(sa-LAAT), or the five daily prayers*
- Sawm *(SO-um), or fasting during Ramadan*
- Zakat *(za-KAT), or giving to charity*
- Hajj *(HAAJ), or journeying to Mecca.*

day is a big sacrifice. When Ramadan falls in the summer, a daily fast may last for twelve hours because the days are longer.

Fasting during Ramadan helps Muslims appreciate how lucky they are to have enough food to eat every day.

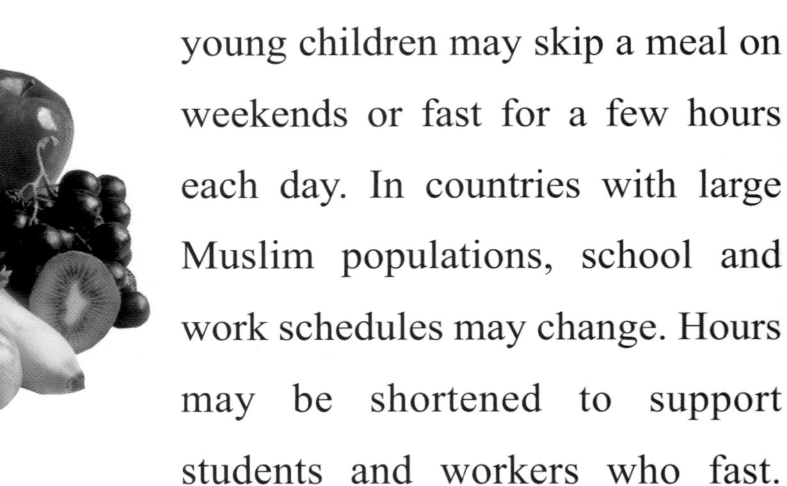

Children do not have to fast all month until they are teenagers. In some Muslim families, young children may skip a meal on weekends or fast for a few hours each day. In countries with large Muslim populations, school and work schedules may change. Hours may be shortened to support students and workers who fast. Sacrifice is part of what Ramadan is about. It helps Muslims appreciate how lucky they are to have enough food to eat every day. It reminds them that others are not so lucky.

Another Ramadan duty is *Zakat* (za-KAT). Zakat is giving money to help the poor. Some

Another part of Ramadan is giving money to help the poor.

children who do not fast give their allowance to the poor, instead. Thinking of others is part of the Ramadan spirit.

Once night falls, Muslim cities come alive. After night prayers, Ramadan becomes a time for food and fun. A snack of dates and water is eaten to break the fast. Then, a large evening meal called *iftar* (if-TAAR) is served.

Cafes and restaurants that were closed during the day reopen at night. They fill with hungry customers. Hotels may set up outdoor tents with popular foods and fruit drinks. There may be music and dancing. Families and friends visit each other and have parties and get-togethers. Sports such as soccer and rugby are played in lighted fields or in the streets.

In some Muslim cultures, meals like this are prepared for the iftar.

TV and radio stations broadcast special Ramadan programs. In Egypt and the United Arab Emirates, one of these programs is called the "Fawazeer Ramadan," (fa-WAA-zeer ra-ma-DAAN) or "Ramadan Riddles." It is a variety show, with big musical numbers and costumed folk dance routines. Top performers act out riddles, and prizes are awarded. There is one riddle for each night of Ramadan.

Some people play soccer to enjoy the festivities.

In Bangladesh, a young couple participates in the Eid ul-Fitr festivities. Here they are wearing the costumes of a king and queen.

CHAPTER 5

Eid Festivities

When Ramadan ends on the first day of the month of Shawwaal, *Eid ul-Fitr* (EED-ul-FIT-er) begins. The Eid is a three-day festival to celebrate a successful fast. Sky watchers once again watch for a crescent moon. When a crescent appears, the new month has arrived. In rural villages in Yemen, fires are lit to announce the joyful Eid tidings. Families then prepare for community Eid prayers. They dress in new clothes, shoes, and headscarves. Women may stain their skin with henna in swirling patterns. Men may get haircuts or shave their heads altogether.

MUSLIM FLAG

The bright green flag bears a crescent moon and a star, a common symbol of Islam. It has been used by various Muslim nations. Royal blue and gold are also associated with Islam. They represent the colors of the night sky.

Many countries, including Pakistan, whose flag is seen here, include the crescent moon and star to show their faith.

After prayers, gifts are exchanged. Neighbors and friends bring each other wrapped cakes, nuts, and strings of dried fruit such as figs, dates, apricots, and raisins. They congratulate each other for completing the fast. *Eid Mubarak* (EED moo-BAA-rek), they say. Happy Festival!

During Eid, children go from house to

In Nepal, Muslim girls decorate their hands with henna. Henna is a reddish-brown natural dye from henna leaves.

house collecting money, sweets, and candy. Turkish delight, or *lokum* (lo-CAM), is a rich, sticky candy that is made in the country of Turkey. It is one of the oldest candies in the world. Cooks in the palace of the sultan created this sweet in the eighteenth century. Sugar syrup, pistachio, hazelnut, coconut, orange, and rosewater are some of its interesting flavors. Legends say that lokum is so good that it can make you forget all that you know!

In countries like Pakistan, there are street fairs with balloons and carnival games. Street vendors, people who offer goods for sale, paint their carts bright green, blue, and gold. They add symbols such as stars and

Gifts of dates and figs are given to neighbors to celebrate the end of the fast.

The shops in Lebanon sell decorations for Ramadan.

crescent moons to represent Islam. There may be parades with sword-dancing and drums.

Wherever Muslims gather to celebrate Eid, it is a time for relaxation and merriment. Communities make sure that everyone, including the poor, is well fed and content. Muslims around the world happily give thanks to God for their health, their strength, and their opportunities in life.

Muslim families give thanks to God for their health, strength, and opportunities in life. This family lives in the United Kingdom.

Ramadan Craft Project

Stars and Moons Garland

Ramadan starts when we see a crescent moon in the ninth month of the Islamic calendar. Make a Ramadan decoration using the moon and stars.

You will need:

- ✔ **tracing paper**
- ✔ **10 sheets of white paper**
- ✔ **gold crayons or markers**
- ✔ **silver crayons or markers**
- ✔ **scissors**
- ✔ **hole punch**
- ✔ **8 feet of string or yarn**

1. Trace the star pattern on the next page using tracing paper. Cut out the traced star pattern. Trace as many stars as you can fit onto a sheet of paper. Color the stars using a gold crayon or marker. Cut out all the stars. Do the same thing with the moon pattern. Color the moons with a silver crayon or marker and cut them out.

2. Using the hole punch, punch a small hole near the top of each star and each moon.

3. String one star, then one moon onto yarn. Space the stars and moons evenly.

4. Ask an adult to help you hang your Ramadan decoration over a door.

Words to Know

calligraphy—An elegant, artistic style of handwriting.

decree—A religious order.

Islam—The religious faith of Muslims that is based on the belief in one God, known in Arabic as *Allah*.

mosque—A building used by Muslims for public worship; comes from the Arabic word *masjid*.

Muslim—A believer in the religion of Islam.

prophet—A person who delivers a message that is believed to have come from God.

Qur'an—The book of sacred writings accepted by Muslims as revelations from God.

revelation—Something that is revealed by God to humans.

ritual—An established religious ceremony.

scribe—A person who copies writing.

sermon—A religious speech.

worship—To honor or to show respect to God or to a sacred object.

Reading About

Douglass, Susan L. *Ramadan*. Minneapolis, Minn.: Lerner Publishing Group, 2003.

Hoyt-Goldsmith, Diane. *Celebrating Ramadan*. New York: Holiday House, Inc., 2002.

Ross, Mandy. *Mecca*. Austin, Tex.: Raintree Publishers, 2003.

Walsh, Kieran. *Ramadan*. Vero Beach, Fla.: Rourke Publishing, LLC., 2002.

Internet Addresses

COUNCIL ON ISLAMIC EDUCATION

<http://www.cie.org/>

Learn more about Ramadan and other Islamic holidays.

MUHAMMAD

<http://www.pbs.org/empires/islam/profilesmuhammad.html>

Learn more about the Prophet of Islam, Muhammad.

RAMADAN ON THE NET

<http://www.holidays.net/ramadan>

Find out more about Ramadan from this Web site.

Index

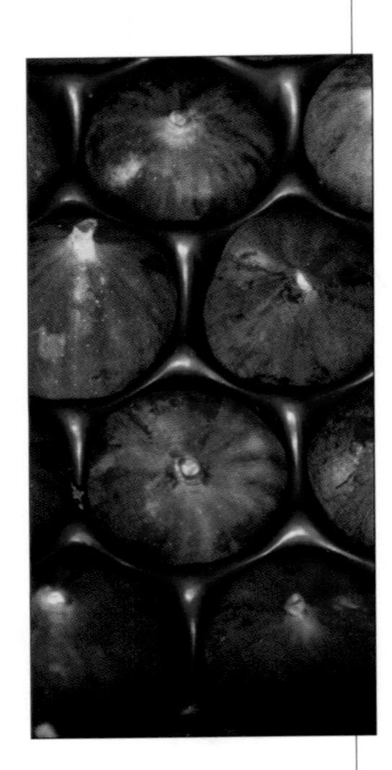